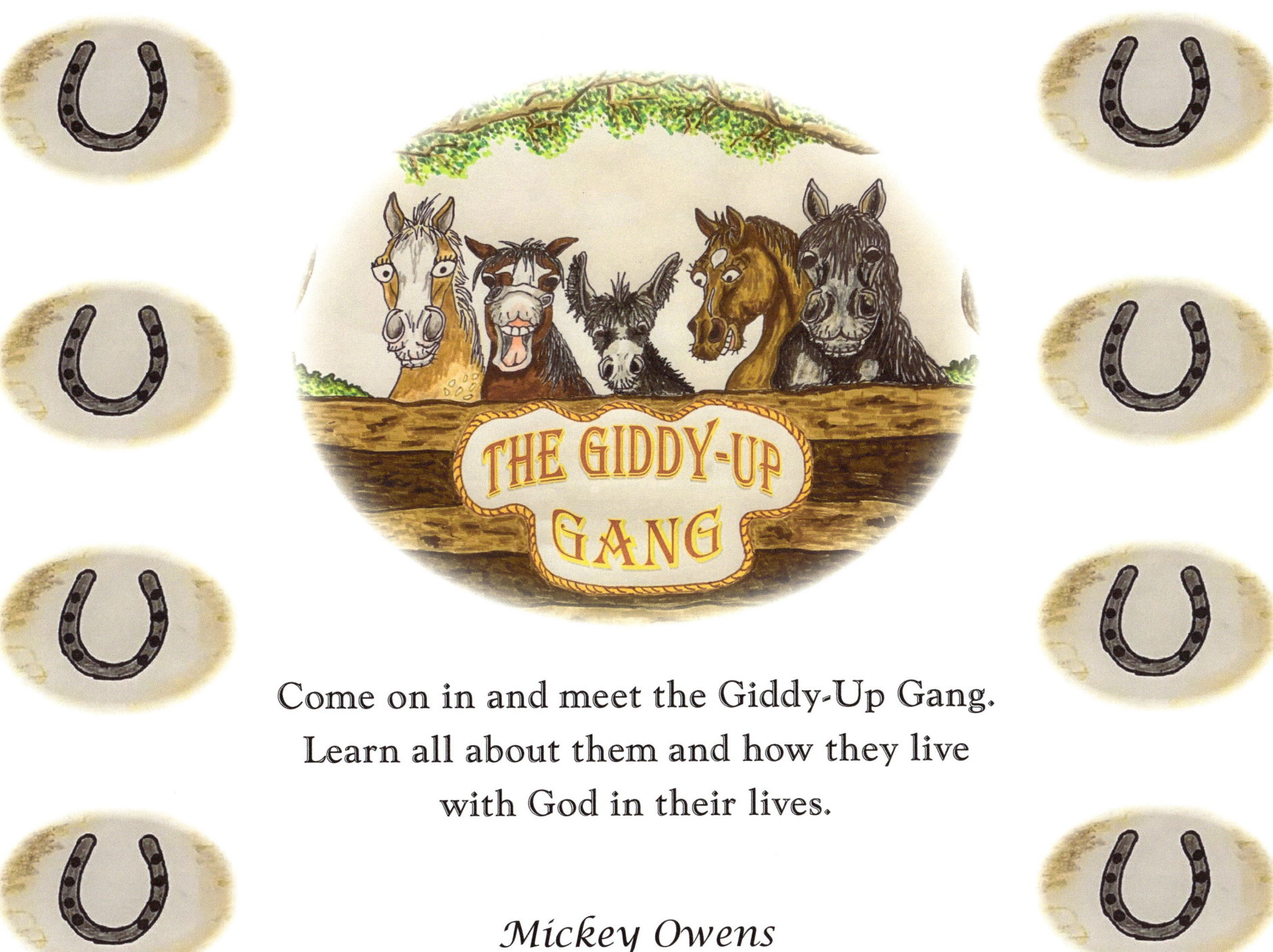

Come on in and meet the Giddy-Up Gang.
Learn all about them and how they live
with God in their lives.

Mickey Owens

ISBN 979-8-9866879-0-2 (hardback)
ISBN 979-8-9866879-1-9 (paperback)
ISBN 979-8-9866879-2-6 (digital)

Copyright © Mickey Owens 2022

All rights reserved. No part of this publication may be reproduced, distributed, or transmitted in any form or by any means, including photocopying, recording, or other electronic or mechanical methods without the prior written permission of the publisher. For permission requests, solicit the publisher via the address below.

Mickey Owens
1010 County Road 307
McDade, TX 78650

Printed in the United State of America

The author assumes no responsibility or liability for any errors or omissions in the content of this book. The information shared is intended to help entertain, educate and inform the reader. The ultimate success or failure of this shared information will be the result of the reader's own efforts and innumerable other circumstances beyond author's control. This author wishes to thank the real life characters used in this book.

Acknowledgements

This has been my first attempt at self-publishing. If you are reading this,
I'm assuming it was successful. This has certainly not been an easy journey,
but if it touches the heart of one person, I will have been greatly rewarded.

I have been blessed by the support of some very special people.

Thanks to my sister Yvonne and sister-in-law Carla for never wavering in their
efforts to encourage me to take the first step of writing and publishing this book.

Many thanks to my "sister-pack" lady friends:

Alexis, Beverly, Lori, Misty and Nancy

They have encouraged and provided me the motivation to complete this journey.

Lastly, thanks to all the people who purchased my first book
and kept asking when this one would be completed.

God has always gifted me with angels in my life.

I thank Him for that priceless gift.

A final thank you to the stars of this book...

Listo, Rascal, Deets, Cooper and Vato

My name is Listo. That is a Spanish word that means "ready". I look very different from the other horses because I am an Appaloosa. We have spots and lots of different colors.

BEAUTY

God reminds us that beauty comes in many forms.
Thank you God for making me unique and different.
Always remember that beauty is God's handwriting
and it's always perfect.

I praise you because you made me in an amazing and wonderful way.
What you have done is wonderful. I know this very well.
Psalm 139:14 NCV

Life Changes

Even though things don't stay the same, help me to remember that change brings with it hope for better things ahead.

And I will hope in your name, For your name is good.
Psalm 52:9

My name is Rascal. I got that name because I always seem to misbehave. I can be grouchy sometimes so I often just hang out by myself.

Choose Good Choices

Life is all about choices. We can always ask God to help us make good choices. We can choose to be angry, but choose to find joy. We can choose to be idle, but we can choose to do good things. We can choose to be selfish and self-indulgent, but instead choose to give. We can choose to get even, but instead choose to forgive.

Get rid of all bitterness, rage and anger, brawling and slander, along with every form of malice. Be kind and compassionate to one another, forgiving each other, just as in Christ, God forgave you.
Ephesians 4:31-32

My name is Cooper. I am a Quarter Horse. We are born to run very fast! I love to race with the birds. They are my friends.

Your Race

When you run a race in life, it encourages others to join you. The goal always is to finish your race. Not to be first . . . but to just finish. As you run, you can cheer each other on and help each other if you fall. God loves to see you run His race.

Let us run with perseverance the race marked out for us, fixing our eyes on Jesus, our leader and instructor of faith.
Hebrews 12:1-2

My name is Deets. I am a donkey and I look different than the horses. I'm much smaller than them and my ears are much bigger. Even though I'm not beautiful, I'm still pretty darn cute! Because I am small, I can't walk as fast as them. So, I have to trot to keep up. I'm always the last in line.

God Loves Different

So do you find that you don't quite fit in? You might even stick out like a sore thumb. Don't ever be afraid to stand out. Be bold and proud of how God has made you. That's what God loves to see.

On the day I called out to you, you answered me.
You made me strong and brave.
Psalm 138:3

God's Clothes

God, help us to learn the importance of our clothing. Please guide our choices of dress so that we are a reflection of You.

"Adorn yourself with eminence and dignity,
and clothe yourself with honor and majesty."
Job 40:10

Sometimes we try to impress each other. I like to show Rascal how good I can prance. Rascal likes to show off his beautiful mane and tail.

Your Gift

God has given each of us different gifts and talents.
We can use our God-given ability to take something
ordinary and make it into something special.
Don't be afraid to show your talents to others.
God loves the flair that you can add to His world.

Each man has his own gift from God; one has this gift, another has that.
1 Corinthians 7:7

When it gets hot outside, we love to go swimming. We are very big, but we can swim very fast! We paddle with our four feet. God gives us nice clean water that we can drink. So it's very important to keep it that way.

God's World

Thank you God for the beauty found in your world. It is like a secret garden that we can enjoy and find pleasure in. Help us to see your wonder in the beauty that surrounds us.

Ah, Lord God! It is you who have made the heavens and the earth by your great power and by your outstretched arm! Nothing is too hard for you.
Jeremiah 32:17

And, "You Lord, laid the foundation of the earth in the beginning, and the heavens are the work of your hands."
Hebrews 1:10

Travel with God

God, please be my GPS in my travels. Help me to remember that difficult roads often lead to beautiful destinations. Keep me safe by being my guide and giving me direction.

Your word is a lamp to guide my feet and a light for my path.
Psalm 119:105

Have Fun

God, you have taught us that we should learn to enjoy life. We should bring joy and laughter to those around us. Humor helps heal wounds and teaches us that you like laughter too.

You have turned for me my mourning into dancing; You have loosened my sack cloth and gave me festive garments to rejoice in.
Psalm 30:11

You have made known to me the path of life; in your presence there is fullness and joy; at your right hand are pleasures forevermore.
Psalm 16:11

God Sent a Friend

There is no friend like the friend who shares your mornings, welcomes your embrace, prays with you in the moonlight, and shares the magic moments of Life.

My command is this: Love each other as I have loved you.
John 15:12

There are "friends" who pretend to be friends,
but there is a friend who sticks closer than a brother.
Proverbs 18:24

Just like you, we wear shoes too!
But, ours are different from yours.
Our shoes are made out of metal
and fit on the bottom of our foot.
A man called a farrier attaches them
with small nails that don't hurt.
Our shoes keeps rocks from hurting
the tender part of our foot.

God Gives Protection

God is our rock and we can trust Him to provide
protection from the pain in this world.
We can surrender ourselves to His caring
and capable hands.

The Lord keeps you from all harm and watches over your life.
The Lord keeps watch over you as you come and go, both now and forever.
Psalm 121:7-8

Even though we are horses, we have a dentist too! He comes to our barn and takes care of our teeth. We are not afraid because he is very gentle and he doesn't hurt us.

God's Caregivers

God, when we need to stay healthy, You send us angels of mercy who provide care and support to us. It is through them that we see Your loving hand.

"He went to him and bound up his wounds, pouring on oil and wine.
Then he set him on his own animal and brought him to an inn
and took care of him."
Luke 10:34

On hearing this, Jesus said, "It is not the healthy who
need a doctor, but the sick."
Matthew 9:12

With God, We Can Face Our Fears

Many things in this world may frighten us, but God will give us the strength to face them with power and love. God is aware of each and every fear we have. . . even the most hidden ones.

For the Holy Spirit, God's gift, does not want you to be afraid,
but to be wise and strong and to love everyone.
2 Timothy 1:7

God's Hotline

When we pick up our prayer "phone", it goes straight to God. His hotline is never tied up or busy. The Lord will pick up and you'll have His undivided attention. Through prayer, you can bring all your tears, fears, regrets, and requests and at the same time acknowledge all the mighty things He has done in your life.

The Lord is near to all who call on him, to all who call on him in truth.
Psalm 145:18

Then you will call on Me and come and pray to Me, and I will listen to you.
Jeremiah 29:12

At the end of each day, we all go towards the barn . . . our home.
It will be time to eat our dinner and go to sleep.
We have a special secret . . . We can sleep standing up.

End of the Day . . . Going Home

Did you learn how God works in your life?
Did you learn about beauty, change, choices, running your race, loving yourself, talents, joy, reflecting God, direction in life, friendships and love, mercy, trust, facing fears, God's secret garden, and prayer? If God is working in your life, tell someone!

"The living, the living—they praise you, as I am doing today; parents tell their children about your faithfulness". Isaiah 38:19

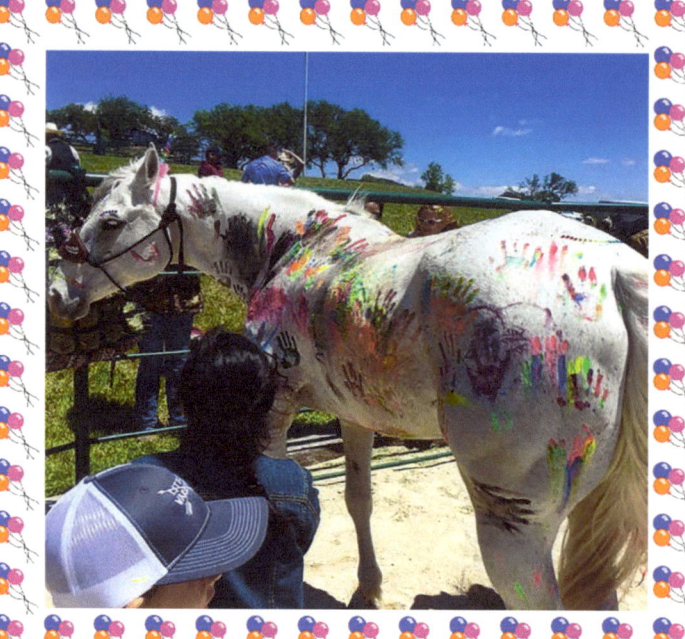

Little Warriors

These are children, recovering from cancer, participating in one of the fun activities associated with horses. It lets them exhibit their creativities and enjoy a day full of fun that's free of medical restrictions

SPECIAL FUN SECTION

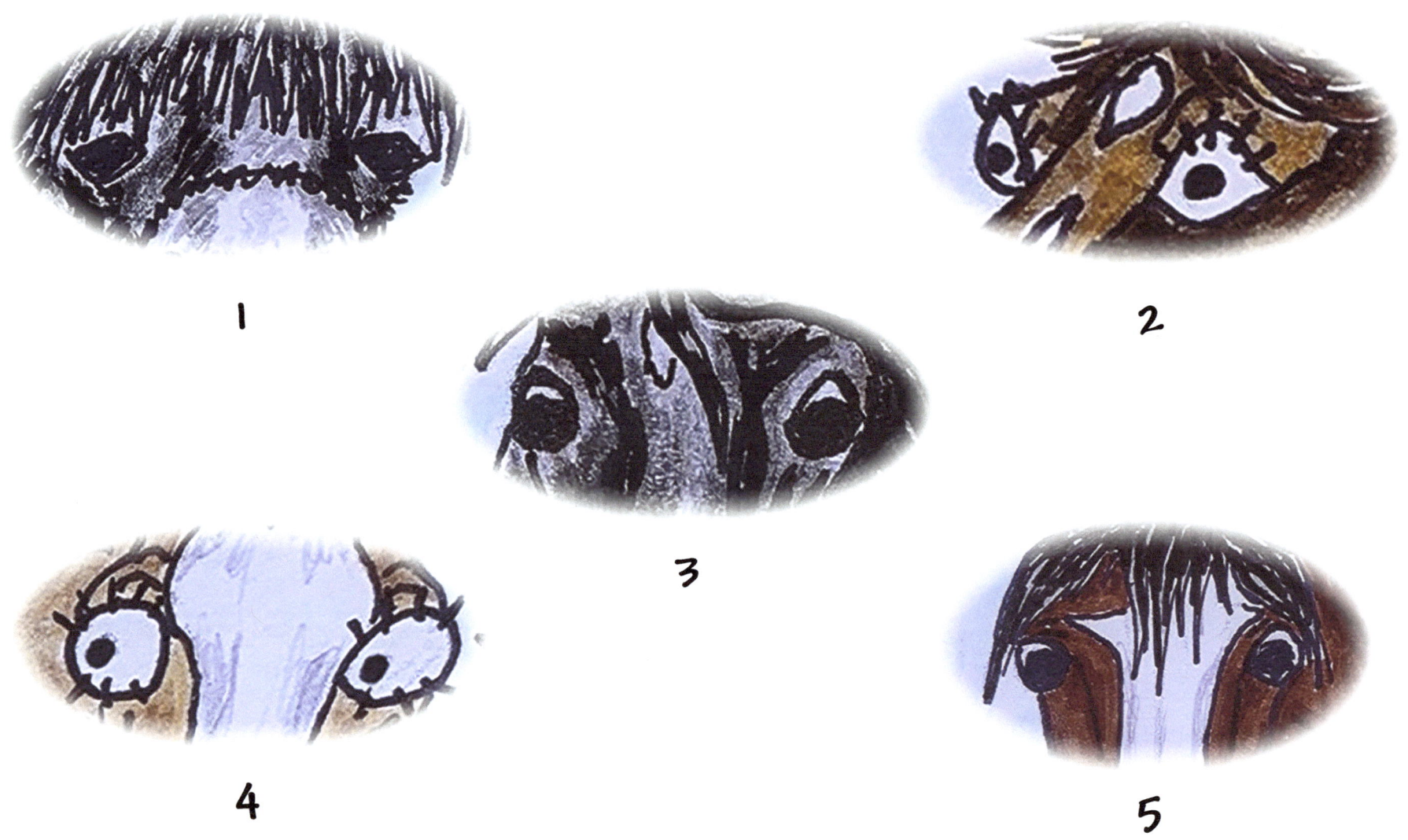

Whose eyes are these?

Write your answers on a piece of paper. Answers on Page 39.

Whose ears are these?

Write your answers on a piece of paper. Answers on Page 39.

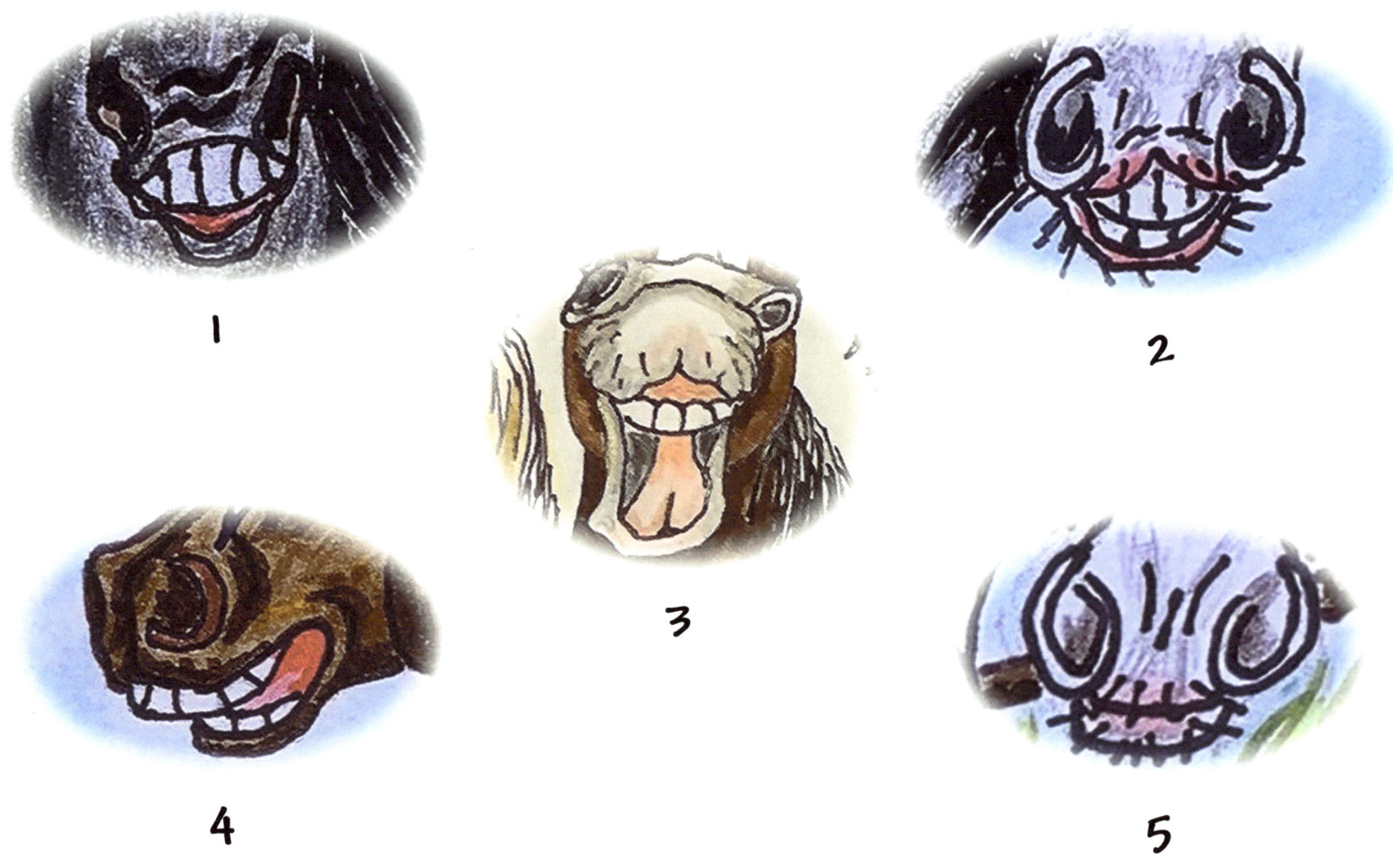

Whose noses are these?

Write your answers on a piece of paper. Answers on Page 39.

About the Author

Mickey Owens is a retired business owner. Her ranch located near Austin, Texas is where she spends most of her time. She has always had an interest in young children and teens. She worked in the youth horsemanship program and the youth bible study at her church. Mickey has also volunteered several years in the Little Warriors program which helps children recovering from cancer by introducing them to the fun found in horses.

Now, she has discovered a new way to reach out to children by writing a book that teaches them about horses and God.

ANSWERS TO FUN PAGES

Eyes

1. Deets   2. Cooper   3. Vato   4. Listo   5. Rascal

Ears

1. Listo   2. Vato   3. Deets   4. Rascal   5. Cooper

Noses

1. Vato   2. Deets   3. Rascal   4. Cooper   5. Listo

We hope that you have enjoyed learning about
The Giddy-Up Gang

Be sure to watch for future stories about
our exciting new adventures.

www.ingramcontent.com/pod-product-compliance
Lightning Source LLC
Chambersburg PA
CBHW042135060526

44119CB00116B/359